Preaching the Word
(Second Edition)

A Guide to Expository Preaching

by

Paul Smith

A met Publication

© 2014 Methodist Evangelicals Together

Published on behalf of MET by

MOORLEYS
Print & Publishing
tel: 0115 932 0643 web: www.moorleys.co.uk

© Copyright 2014 MET

ISBN 978 0 86071 682 2
(First Edition Published as 0 86071 524 8 in 1998)

All rights reserved.
No part of this publication may be reproduced, stored in a retrieval system, or transmitted, in any form or by any means, electronic, mechanical, photocopying, recording or otherwise, without the prior written permission of the publishers.

British Library Cataloguing in Publication Data.
A catalogue record for this book is available from the British Library.

Published on behalf of MET by

tel: 0115 932 0643 web: www.moorleys.co.uk

Foreword

"You will see from the preface that this little book first appeared last century! I have been deeply encouraged to learn that it has been a help to many and that a re-print is now required. So here it is. Its original publication came at a time when there was an increased interest in preaching. I am glad to say that since that time the interest has continued, if not increased. So it is offered once more in the hope that it may be of some help to those who have known God's call to this high office and who seek to be better equipped for the task.

It has been my great privilege to preach the gospel for over forty years and even though I have now retired from pastoral ministry I preach regularly in the local area and beyond. I will continue to do so as long as He lends me breath, for there is no greater calling.

> Happy if with my latest breath
> I might but gasp His name,
> Preach Him to all and cry in death
> Behold! Behold the Lamb.

Paul Smith, 2014
Bere Alston
Devon

Preface

For many years the Christian Church suffered from a lack of confidence in preaching. When I was a student I remember speaking to a much older Methodist Minister about preaching. He told me that he thought preaching was like throwing a bucket of water over a crate of empty milk bottles. You may get a bit it here and there, but it was not the most effective way of fulfilling your ministry. The illustration spoke volumes about his lack of confidence. Sunday by Sunday he was required to preach, and all the while he did not really believe in what he was doing. Such a situation did not strengthen the faith of either the preacher or the congregation. Yet there were many preachers who shared his lack of confidence.

Gladly, that has changed. Our generation has seen an increased interest in the preacher's task. The Church is once again beginning to believe that preaching can make a difference. We now have preaching conferences where the more experienced preachers share their insights with those who are less experienced. The College of Preachers does a fine job in promoting this God-given task. There is a new awareness that preaching is God's chosen way for proclaiming the good news of Jesus and unfolding the truth of His word. We do not deny the effectiveness of other methods of Christian communication, yet we acknowledge that preaching occupies a unique position in the economy of God. All those who have sat under great preaching know its power. It is through preaching that so often conviction is wrought in the soul. It is through preaching that the wonder of God's grace is set forth for all to experience. It is through preaching that followers of Jesus are drawn closer to Him.

This little book is offered to all who know God's call to this great task with the prayer that it may be of some help to them as they seek to fulfil their ministry. If you have bought this book, borrowed it, or even just picked it up and read this far, the chances are that you are a preacher who wants to preach better. You can! No matter how long you have been preaching, or how experienced you are, there is always room for improvement. The people who never get any better at preaching are the people who do not really want to! If you have the desire and if you share a vision for this ministry you already posses the two basic requirements for any who would be a better preacher of the Gospel.

Unfortunately, in English, pronouns have to be either male, female or neuter. Throughout this book the male pronoun has been used. To say "he or she" or "s/he" on every occasion makes for clumsy textual flow. To opt for "he" in one chapter and "she" in the next smacks of tokenism. "He", therefore, ought to be understood to refer to the preacher of either gender. I record, with gratitude, my debt to all those preachers, male and female, who have enabled me to encounter God through His word. When it comes to preaching what matters is not whether the preacher is male or female, but whether they are called of God, filled with His Spirit and, through diligent study and preparation, equipped to fulfil this high calling.

Paul Smith
September 1998

The Preacher's Calling and Resources

People describe preaching in different ways. For some the idea of explanation is most important. For others any preaching worthy of the name ought to challenge the hearer. Others will emphasise a simple setting forth of the gospel message and others will stress the fact that all preaching ought to offer Christ to the hearer. All these aspects of preaching are important, but none really answer the question 'What is Preaching?'

Phillips Brooks defined preaching as 'truth through personality'. He reminds us of two complementary truths. In the first place the preacher is concerned with truth. Biblical preaching is not primarily concerned with sharing an opinion, but setting forth truth. The preacher does not give the congregation a concept which is up for debate. He lays the truth of God's word before them. Secondly, such truth is communicated through the preacher's personality. Let's not fight shy of this. Ours is an incarnational faith. When God wanted to reach a lost world he did so through the personality of Jesus. Is it surprising that He should choose to reach a congregation through the personality of the preacher? Of course, a strong personality alone is not enough. Strong personality and weak theology lead to personality cults and heresy. But if the personality of the preacher is yielded to Christ we ought not to be surprised that he is able to use it as a vehicle for communicating the good news of Jesus.

B.L. Manning offers another definition. 'Preaching,' he says, 'is the manifestation of the incarnate Word, from the written word, by the spoken word.' Christ-centred biblical exposition delivered in the language and thought forms of the hearers has a power which only God can give. Such an understanding offers a way of evaluating our own preaching, as well as that of others. Did the spoken word really communicate what was in the preacher's mind? Was it from the written word? For only truly biblical preaching can have the authority which belongs to scripture alone. Was the incarnate Word, our Lord Jesus Christ, manifest through the message of the preacher in such a way that the congregation encountered Him?

Fred Craddock of Emery University, Atlanta offers us another way of looking at preaching. He reminds us that the preacher's task is not to say what the congregation wants to hear but to say what the congregation wants to say if they could only say it! The gospel which the preacher expounds must have that ring of truth about it, which resonates with every believer's heart. We all recognise that to be true. How many there are who have thought, as they walked home after hearing great preaching, 'I wish I had said that!' It was not just that the content of the preaching brought some new insight but that the preacher wonderfully expressed some profound truth which stirred the hearer at the core of his being.

These definitions remind us of the contrast between preaching and both lecturing and oratory. The purpose of a lecture is to impart information. If the preacher believes that this is his primary task his preaching will be dull and lifeless, like many lectures. He will be perceived as trying to make his congregation into students, and many will resent it. They will be kind. As they shake his hand they will say, 'That was interesting' or, 'That was a bit deep this morning' and he will know that he may have stimulated the mind but he has missed the heart, let alone the will. If, on the other hand, the preacher believes that his primary task is to 'move' his congregation he will place more emphasis on the oratory which accompanies his delivery than the substance of the message. They may be moved, but they will not grow. Such preaching may draw a crowd of shallow Christians for a while, but before long they will become dissatisfied. If they really encounter Christ they will need feeding, and oratory alone is insufficient to meet their need. True preaching is neither lecturing nor oratory. It is a God-ordained way of encountering people with the truth of the gospel, and such an encounter will stimulate the mind, warm the heart and challenge the will.

'Then', one might ask, 'who is equal to such a task and what are the resources on which the preacher can draw?' We need to be clear about two things -

The Preacher's Call
Firstly, there is only one essential qualification for the preacher. It is the call of God. The individual does not decide to be a preacher. God decides who He is going to call. He chooses whoever He will and bestows a power to enable the task to be performed to His glory. Like Jeremiah, every preacher must have a sense that God is calling him to this great task (Jer 1:4-10). Like Ezekiel he must be aware that he is being sent with a divine message (Ezek 2:1-4). Like Isaiah he must yield to the call in glad obedience, unworthy though he is (Is 6:8).

The disciples knew it too. They were called to follow Christ (Matt 4:19) with the promise that they would become fishers of men. Before long they were sent by Him to preach the good news of the Kingdom (Matt 10:5-8). They did not choose to go. They went because they were called and sent. It is clear that such a commissioning had a profound effect on them. Peter bears testimony to it (Acts 10:42). Paul knew it too (Acts 16:10) and saw it as a tremendous privilege (Eph 3:7&8). It is the call of God alone which makes a person a preacher. Without this all his effort is in vain... Dr. Martin Lloyd Jones puts it like this,
> 'What about preaching....There is only one thing to say about this; it cannot be taught. That is impossible. Preachers are born not made. This is an absolute. You will never teach a man to be a preacher if he is not one already. All books such as 'A.B.C of Preaching' or 'Preaching made Easy' should be thrown onto the fire as soon as possible.'

Secondly, whilst the call of God is the preacher's essential equipment, that does not excuse him from using every available resource to equip himself for the task. Indeed, if he really knows the call of God he will want to do all he can to fulfil his ministry to the best of his ability. Preachers who are able to sustain a ministry know all too well how much preparation is involved. To ignore the study required in the mistaken belief that having known God's call he will receive the inspiration needed when he gets into the pulpit is to fundamentally misunderstand the grace of God. Effective preaching needs both preparation and inspiration, and often perspiration too!

Conscious of the importance of the preacher's task, we need to examine the resources on which he can draw to enable him to fulfil his ministry. We will consider both the spiritual and the material resources at his disposal.

Spiritual resources
The Authority of Scripture is the expository preacher's primary resource. He is aware that the Bible brings an authority which cuts to the heart of the hearer (Heb.4:12). If the preacher can enable an encounter between the hearer and God's word he will find that God's word will do its own work. The preacher's vital task is to bring the Bible to the people and the people to the Bible.

Paul was convinced of *the power of the Gospel* (Rom 1:16), and the preacher too can see this as a resource which God has provided. The gospel, God's gracious message to a lost world, brings its own convicting power. It has a ring of truth for all who hear it, and as it is faithfully proclaimed the preacher will find that it does its own work in the hearts of his hearers, almost apart from him.

The power of the Holy Spirit (Acts 1:8, 5:32) ought to be active in every aspect of the preacher's ministry. It will be the Holy Spirit who aids the preacher's preparation, enabling him to grasp the truth of scripture. As the message is proclaimed the Holy Spirit will endue the preacher with a power not his own. As the message is heard the Holy Spirit will apply it to the life of the hearer bringing about His own convicting and constraining work. Every preacher needs to receive the 'power from on high' which Jesus promised (Luke 24:49).

Nor should the preacher ignore *the prayer support of God's people*. Paul asked the Ephesian Christians to pray for him (Eph 6:19&20) and no preacher should be too proud to ask other Christians for their prayer support. It is a wonderful thing to declare the word of God knowing that other Christians are praying for you.

When the aged Paul wrote to the young Timothy he was anxious to encourage him in his ministry (2 Tim 4:1-5). Every preacher should know *the encouragement of other preachers* as he seeks to fulfil his calling.

All these spiritual resources, together with *the absolute dedication to the task in hand* (Rom 1:15, 1 Cor 9:16) should enable the preacher to feel that, demanding though his task is, all the resources of God and God's people are supporting him.

Material Resources

We must now consider the material resources which the preacher can use. Some of these will be dealt with in greater detail later, but at this point we simply note them.

The Bible is the preacher's primary material resource. Like Wesley, the expository preacher will endeavour to be 'a man of one book'. Of course he will read other literature, but it will chiefly be to aid his understanding of scripture and the task of preaching. The expository preacher will grow to know his Bible well. That will involve having a grasp of the 'big picture' of God's self-revelation through scripture, as well as a detailed knowledge of individual stories and books. There is no substitute for a good working knowledge of the scriptures.

Further, the preacher will endeavour to have a grasp of *Christian history and biography*. He will seek to draw on the wealth of illustrative material available as he discovers how God's people down the centuries have responded to, and lived out the gospel.

In addition to this, the serious preacher will always be on the look-out for *quotations and illustrations* which he can use. The good story he hears, the incident which he witnesses, the quotation which he reads; all will provide the material he needs to reinforce Biblical truth and apply it to the hearer's life.

As he gathers the material which may be of use at some future date he will quickly discover the need for a *system in which material can be stored and from which it can be retrieved without difficulty.* He will need a system with which he feels comfortable, and for that reason it is best for each preacher to devise his own.

Many preachers need the personal discipline which is imposed by a *lectionary or preaching scheme.* It is far too easy, especially if the preacher seldom occupies the same pulpit, to rely on sermons which were prepared months or even years ago and which have been preached on many previous occasions. Of course, good sermons can be preached more than once, but to rely too heavily on old material leads to a laziness in the study and a lack of enthusiasm in the pulpit.

Dr. Sangster used to speak of *sermons on the stocks*. He was aware that the preacher may come across a text or biblical story which speaks to him during his own devotional reading; but it may not be appropriate for the next occasion when he is going to preach. Rather than lose it the astute preacher will make a note to which he can later return when time allows him to give it more consideration. Over a period of time he may amass quite a collection of such material. He will keep coming back to it, giving each one a little more thought until eventually a sermon, or a number of sermons begin to take shape. In that way he will always have something 'on the stocks' and be saved from that most difficult question 'What am I going to preach on next Sunday?'

Having clarified our understanding of preaching, considered the preacher's call and reminded ourselves of the spiritual and material resources on which the preacher can draw we are now in a position to turn our attention to the task which lies before every preacher of the gospel.

The Preacher's Task

The most common New Testament words for preacher are KERUSSO (κηρυσσω) and KERUX (κηρυξ). Both originally signified a herald. As such the preacher is a messenger with authority. He is one who delivers faithfully that which is not his own; and his message, by implication, demands a response. Any idea of the preacher being one who shares his own opinions, which are then up for debate amongst the congregation, is quite foreign to the biblical understanding of our task. New Testament preaching involved the announcement of facts. God has spoken decisively in Jesus. The preacher proclaimed this message. It was not his own invention. He was merely delivering the truth of what God had done. His hearers were then left wondering what they were to do with it! What was their reasonable and fitting response to such a startling revelation. When they asked, 'What must we do?' the preacher was ready with a clear answer that enabled them to enter into the new life which Christ offers to all. Such preaching did not merely stir the emotions of the hearers or enlighten their intellect. It addressed the whole person with such challenging truth that it demanded a verdict from them. They could no longer remain neutral, for God had stepped into history in Jesus and stepped into their lives through the preacher's message. The purpose of such preaching is crystal clear. It was designed to effect a change in the will, and consequently the direction of the lives of all who heard the message. This is the model for all truly biblical preaching.

But how does the preacher do it? One helpful way of reflecting upon the preacher's task is to see him as a bridge builder. He is required to build two bridges if his preaching is to be effective.

Bridge number one spans the gap between the Bible and the preacher. The world of the New Testament is very different from the one we occupy today. The language is different. The thought forms are different. The culture is different. The customs are different. No preacher worthy of the name can ignore these differences. They represent a gulf between the world which the apostles occupied and our own. When we consider the Old Testament we realise that the gulf is even greater, because the contrast between that society and ours is greater. But if the truth of scripture is really going to live for the preacher, let alone the congregation, it is a gulf which the preacher must bridge.

Building such a bridge involves the preacher in discovering as much as possible about the world of the passage from which he is preaching, and about the passage itself. There are basic questions which every preacher will ask when he turns to a biblical passage. Initially he will have to work through them one by one, but before long it will become second nature to approach the passage in this way. He will endeavour to do all he can to 'get inside' the text, and that will involve getting inside the mind of the one who wrote it and the mind of those who first read it. What did it mean for them? The preacher's answer to that question reveals the kernel of truth which it is the preacher's calling to deliver.

So as he comes to a passage of scripture, the preacher will be asking;
Who wrote this and what were the circumstances which caused it to be written? To or for whom was it written? What can I know about the situation of those who received it or first read it? What was the intention of the writer? What effect did he want this passage to have on those who first read it? Why did the writer include this particular passage in this book?

The preacher will then begin to see the passage in a wider context. How does this truth relate to the passages immediately around it? Is it one episode in an unfolding story? How does it relate to the rest of scripture? How does it relate to God's self-revelation in Christ? What social customs and cultural norms do I need to understand in order to make sense of this passage?

All these questions, and the research which they demand, will help the preacher grasp the truth which lies at the heart of that particular passage of scripture. He is beginning to build the first bridge; the bridge between the world of the Bible and his world. It may be helpful at this stage to identify some principles which need to be taken seriously if this bridge is going to bear the weight of biblical authority.

1. Discover what light the rest of scripture has to shed on a passage before applying its truth directly to your own situation. Context is very important. A text without a context is a pretext. To extract a text from its immediate and wider biblical context and apply it to the modern world as a timeless truth is not to emphasise the authority of scripture, it is to undermine it.

2. Remember that Christ is the touchstone. How does the message of this passage square with Him? This question is very important, especially when considering Old Testament passages of scripture. It is worth remembering that whenever the New Testament writers refer to the scriptures they mean the Old Testament, for those are the only scriptures which they had. It was within their pages that the Apostles saw the unfolding story of God's purposes which led to Christ. The Old Testament did not frighten them off, as preachers and we must not feel daunted by it either.

3. Cultural forms must be broken down to general principles before they can be expressed in another culture. Let two examples suffice. Paul encourages Christians to greet each other with a holy kiss. (Rom 16:16, 1 Cor 16:20, 2

Cor 13:12, 1 Th 5:26) Before we can apply that injunction to a different social culture we need to ask what a kiss signified in the culture to which Paul wrote. We then need to identify the equivalent action in the modern world. If a kiss in Paul's society conveyed a different message to a kiss today we need to be aware of the difference and ask what the equivalent action would be today. The preacher undermines the authority of scripture if he merely claims, 'The Bible says....' and ignores what the Bible means.

Paul also required that women's heads be covered in worship (1Cor 11:3ff). Why was that? The preacher must answer that question before applying that text to his own situation. To apply the injunction without attempting to translate it culturally may result in keeping the letter of the law whilst ignoring its spirit.

4. To apply a lesson from a biblical narrative to a modern situation there needs to be an obvious similarity between the biblical and modern situation in more than one respect. For example, if the preacher is going to take the word of Jesus to the rich young ruler, 'Go, sell your possessions and give to the poor..... Then come, follow me' (Matt 19:21), and apply it to his congregation as a clear command of the Lord, he must first establish the similarity between the situation of the rich young ruler and that of the congregation. If the hearer does not recognise that clear relationship he will not acknowledge the authority of the command. He will simply excuse himself by saying, "That was Jesus' word to him; not necessarily to me." To deal with this text effectively the preacher needs to examine the life of the rich young ruler and establish a clear similarity between his circumstances and attitude and those of the congregation. Only then will the congregation accept Jesus' word to him as a word to them.

There is one remaining question which every preacher must ask of every text or passage of scripture. It is the most important question of all and ought to be written in large letters at the top of every sheet of paper on which he makes his preliminary notes - "*What is this passage really about?* That is the question which will enable the preacher to get to the core of biblical truth and it is this truth which he must faithfully deliver to his congregation.

So let's imagine that the preacher has decided on a passage of scripture which he will expound. He has discovered all he can about it, asked the right questions and followed the principles which we have outlined. He has identified the core truth which lies at the heart of this passage of scripture. In fact, he has done all he can to build this first bridge between the Bible and himself. How does he know that he has been successful. There are two questions which he must ask himself to know that the bridge is built –

1. Can I express the truth of this passage in my own language and cultural form?

   By language we mean the form of expression which is normally used within his own culture. Can he retell the story or relate the passage in a way which could be easily understood by someone from the same cultural background?

2. Can I apply this to my own situation?

   When he has discovered what the passage is <u>really</u> about, the core truth at the heart of the passage, he must ask what that truth means in his own situation and circumstances.

If he can answer both these questions satisfactorily he knows that the first bridge has been built. But that's only the first bridge! The second is the bridge between the preacher and the congregation. If the preacher comes from the same cultural group as the congregation he will not find the second bridge difficult to build. He will know his people well and be able to identify with their way of thinking, their hopes, dreams and disappointments. But he ought not to assume that this is so, without considering this second bridge at all. Many congregations contain a mixture of sub-cultures. Young people use different language to older people, they think differently and have different value systems. They may use the same words, but the words may have different meanings. If you doubt this just watch a television programme which is targeting the youth culture. Words like 'cool' and 'wicked' have quite different meanings in different cultural contexts. If the preacher is going to communicate effectively he must do so in the language of the cultural group he is addressing. However, he should bear in mind that if he deliberately uses words or phrases which his hearers know do not belong to his culture, in order to communicate effectively, it can sound very patronizing. He needs to find a way of speaking naturally but, at the same time, communicating effectively. Often an illustration or a simple word of explanation is all that is needed. Christian jargon must, of course, be avoided. The challenge of building this second bridge becomes clear when we remember that even words which lie at the heart of the gospel message can have quite different meanings for those who do not belong to a Christian culture. The word 'love' is a clear case in point. In secular society today 'love' has a quite different meaning to that understood in Christian circles. Any good communicator will recognise this and avoid the word, unless he makes *his* understanding clear to the hearer by either explanation or illustration.

There are other sub-groups within many congregations. Just think about the congregation which you know best. There may be young and old, rich and poor, married and single, nuclear families and single-parent families. The diligent preacher will always be asking himself, 'How can I relate this truth to them in a way which they will both understand and accept?' At first sight the second bridge may seem easier to build than the first, but on closer examination the preacher can easily discover that the building of the second bridge, between himself and the congregation, can be just as challenging.

One other matter needs to be made clear before we move on. We need to remember the difference between the first bridge and the second. The first bridge is from the Bible to the preacher. All the work done in constructing it is designed to enable the preacher to have a thorough knowledge of the biblical passage and its meaning. In building this bridge the preacher will discover many things which enable him to assimilate the biblical passage and its truth. It is for the preacher's benefit that this bridge has to be constructed.

The second bridge is different. That spans the gulf between preacher and congregation. When building this bridge the preacher's task is to enable his hearers to grasp the core truth of the biblical passage in a way which relates to their own language and cultural situation. His aim is to enable every member of the congregation to leave the service with a clear understanding of what this particular biblical passage means to them in their every-day lives.

A fundamental mistake made by many preachers is to believe that all the material which was used to construct the first bridge ought to be transported over the second! We have all heard preachers like that. They disgorge enough material for twenty sermons. The congregation go home having eaten more than they can digest. To grasp this truth would be to avoid a lot of spiritual indigestion. The preacher needs to build the first bridge to enable him to build the second, but all that is needed to build the first ought not to be carried across the second. The first bridge enables the preacher to understand the heart of the biblical passage. Having grasped that he is in a position to relate the truth to the congregation in a way which is acceptable to them. Yet to do so he does not need to share with them all that he has learned during his preparation. That is for his benefit, not necessarily theirs. He may need to paint a word picture of the cultural situation of the biblical passage to enable them to grasp the core truth; but once they have grasped that truth the preacher must concentrate on illustrating it and applying it so that his congregation can relate to it. That is the only way they will appreciate its relevance for their own situation.

So, in practical terms, how does a preacher handle a biblical passage as he constructs a sermon? It is to this aspect of the preacher's task which we must now turn.

Handling the Text

There are many books which speak of different types of preaching. They will have chapters on Doctrinal Preaching, Topical Preaching, Biographical Preaching, Ethical Preaching etc. Here, however, we are concentrating on expository preaching. It is our conviction that all Christian preaching worthy of the name will involve biblical exposition, even though it may be classified by some in other ways. Our great task is to declare biblical truth and apply it sensitively to the lives of our hearers. Such preaching draws people to Christ, enables Christians to grow in their faith, enriches the life of the preacher and ensures that, no matter how long his ministry may be, he never runs out of material.

Such preaching involves an intimate relationship between the preacher and the biblical text. The word 'text' has traditionally been used to describe the verse of scripture on which the sermon is based. The sermon has often begun with an announcement of the text, together with its reference, before the preacher has commenced his introduction. "My text for this morning is...."

Here we are using the word 'text' in a slightly different way. It may be a single verse of scripture, but it may be a longer passage, a biblical story or even a whole book. Occasionally it can be a single word, but if that is the case the preacher will inevitably wish to speak about the various contexts in which the word is to be found. Sometimes the preacher may wish to bring together a number of scripture verses which deal with a single theme. By text we simply mean the passage of scripture, however short or long, on which the sermon is based.

The text may be 'given' to the preacher, as it is when he follows a lectionary or a planned preaching scheme. This will obviously present the preacher with a challenge, some times more than others, but it ought not to frighten him. If he believes in the inspiration of the whole of scripture, and not just his favourite passages, he must believe that there is a message within that passage which the congregation needs to hear. We are called to declare the whole counsel of God. If the preparation required on such occasions seems demanding the preacher ought to be grateful for all that he is learning in the process. If he offers it to God it will enrich his own soul as well as the souls who compose his congregation.

Sometimes the text will choose the preacher. In his own devotional reading, maybe, he will stumble across some new truth; or some familiar truth will grip his soul with an intensity he has not known before. He will know that he has to preach on it and he will devote the necessary time to grasping that truth so that it can be effectively passed on to the congregation.

Whether the preacher chooses the text, it is chosen for him, or the text chooses the preacher one thing is clear; the text cannot live for the congregation if it has not first lived for the preacher. If it does not immediately set his soul ablaze he will have to work on it until the kindling begins. If the text does not kindle a flame in the preacher's heart it cannot be expected to do so in the hearts of the hearers. Their hearts need to be kindled from his, and his needs to be kindled from the scripture.

In the last chapter we dealt with some of the questions which a preacher must ask as he approaches the text. They will help him understand its context, its meaning for the writer, the original readers and maybe those involved in the incident. Most of all he will seek the core truth which lies at the heart of this passage of scripture. He will keep asking *"What is this <u>really</u> about?"* and only when he has grasped that core truth will he feel able to proceed to construct a sermon.

However, we need to remember that even when the preacher has grasped the core truth of his text he can approach it in different ways. There are two classic methods of approach.

1. The preacher may consider the text as a whole, identify its core truth and use the rest of the sermon to either develop or apply that truth. Such an approach is often called approaching the text from *outside*. The distinctive feature of such an approach is that it works with the text as a whole rather than dividing it up into sections. The points consist of either establishing the truth in the minds of the hearers or applying the implications of the text to their lives.
Let two examples illustrate this kind of sermon.

   In his book 'Westminster Sermons' volume 1 Dr. Sangster has a sermon on Psalm 19:7 'The law of the Lord is perfect'. Throughout the sermon he treats the text as a whole. The substance of the sermon is designed to convince the hearer of the truth of that text. So, he points out in his sub-titles, "Some laws apply only to the people who accept them", "Some laws vary with localities", "Some laws alter with the passing of time" but "The law of the Lord does not change - it is perfect!"

   Or one might imagine a sermon on John 3:16 "For God so loved the world...." One way of handling this text by approaching it from outside would be to ask," What does this truth mean for the world, the church and the individual?" No doubt the preacher would want to speak about the lostness of the world unaware of God's love, the mission of the church sent with His love, the response which that love requires from every individual heart. Yet, for the purposes of our present consideration, the preacher has approached the text from outside and treated it as a whole, elaborating and applying its truth to the lives of the congregation.

2. Alternatively, the preacher may work from *inside* the text. In this case he will certainly not leave the text as a whole. He will rather consider each word or phrase in great detail. If he is preaching from a story he may follow the development of the story or examine the characters involved; but the essential contrast in this method of approach is that the preacher breaks the text into manageable pieces which form the points of his sermon. He does not leave the text as a whole. It is only in the conclusion, after all the pieces have been examined, that the complete text is assembled again so that its composite truth may be hammered home. Again, illustrations may help.

Had Dr. Sangster, working on Psalm 19:7, chosen to work inside the text instead of outside it he may well have dealt with law in his first point, the law of the Lord in his second, and the perfect nature of the law of the Lord in his third; although I am sure that he would have had crisper headings than that!

John 3:16 can also easily be approached in this way. The points may be - God's love, Christ's death, man's choice. The text has been broken down into its salient points and each point has been developed in significant detail.

Sermon Structure

So far we have concentrated on the alternative approaches which we may have to a text. We have assumed, in the examples given above, that whichever approach we adopt it will lead to a sermon with a definite structure. The importance of sermon structure cannot be overstated. As one preacher aptly put it: "Without order in a discourse you cannot get into a subject, and without good order you cannot get out of it!" Structure prevents the preacher rambling on with good material which the congregation cannot accept because they cannot follow him. It also prevents the preacher just rambling on!

However, unless we understand the purpose of sermon structure we may finish up with a sermon where the structure is either far too obvious or insufficient to support the material which we have. Just as every building needs a framework to support it so every sermon needs structure, but how obvious that framework needs to be can be a matter of taste. So, what are we hoping the sermon structure will do?

1. Good structure enables the congregation to remember the points which the preacher makes. The preacher must ask whether it is important for them to remember. In some sermons this is clearly an advantage; If, for example, he is developing an argument to convince the congregation of a truth which he wants them to accept. In other sermons it is quite unnecessary and to spend a long time developing easily memorised titles for his points would clearly be a waste of effort.

2. One other major advantage of clear construction concerns its value not to the congregation but to the preacher. If the preacher is able to develop a clear structure to his sermon he will find his preparation much easier. Indeed, without a clear structure adequate preparation is virtually impossible. It may be quite unnecessary for the congregation to remember his points, but it is essential that he does so! When it comes to the actual delivery of the sermon one cannot over-estimate the value of a clear structure. It enables the preacher to have a clear understanding of where he is going in the sermon and how to get there. As an aid to his memory it is invaluable.

3. There is an altogether different way of approaching sermon structure. It is to see the sermon, not as a building but as a journey. The purpose of such a sermon is to take the congregation with you to your destination. The route you travel is not as important as the destination at which you arrive. In such a case the preacher needs to identify the milestones on the way; they will be his points, but the congregation does not need to identify them at all. Indeed, to do so may well be a distraction from the whole purpose of such a sermon.

So, let us imagine that a text has been selected. As the preacher reflects on both the text and all the background material before him a number of themes will become apparent. These will constitute the main points of the sermon. If he is preaching on a passage rather than a verse or word of scripture the preacher will want to divide it into sections and give each section a title. These titles will provide the headings for the points which he wants to make. At this stage in the operation he will not be too concerned about the precise wording of the title for each point. All he needs is something to provide a framework for the greater structure which the sermon demands.

Once he has got a clear idea of the sermon points the preacher will want to arrange and order them in the way which is going to be most helpful to his congregation and which will enable him, as the preacher, to attain his objective. This stage in the process is very important. Good though the points may be, if the preacher deals with them in the wrong order the impact of the sermon may be lost. We have all heard sermons where the major point came first so that instead of the sermon rising to a crescendo it becomes less and less significant as it proceeds. Some very simple rules about the way points in any sermon or address ought to be arranged will provide invaluable help in enabling the sermon to achieve its objectives. The preacher must remember that -

1. Explanation and argument needs to come before appeal. Every sermon must appeal to the congregation in some way, and consequently demand a response. The most effective sermons lay the foundations for such an appeal by offering whatever explanation is necessary, or establishing the line of argument, before the preacher moves on to appeal for some response from

the congregation. To reverse this order is to lose whatever impact the appeal would have had.

2. Feelings should deepen as the sermon progresses. All effective sermons touch the heart as well as the mind. The preacher is wrestling with profound truth which must move the hearer deeply. The profundity of truth and the depth of feeling which that truth draws from the hearer should deepen as the sermon progresses. The final point is the one in which the deep places in the human heart must be touched if the hearer is going to make an adequate response. To try and touch these places too early in the sermon means that its effectiveness is lost and the congregation have time to recover from any impact which God's truth may have made on them.

3. The weaker thought should always lead to the stronger. As the preacher identifies the points which he wants to make some will, inevitably, be stronger than others. The strong points are those with the most profound truths or the most evocative insights. These are the ones which should come towards the end of the sermon. The weaker points are best used to unfold the text and lead the congregation to the place where the stronger points are able to break upon them with greatest impact.

4. The general point should always lead to the personal. The effective preacher has the hearts of his hearers in his sights from the moment he begins his preparation. The heart of each individual member of the congregation is the target at which he is aiming the arrow of God's truth. If he is to hit the target he needs to concentrate upon it. The focus of the sermon's attention needs to become more personal as the sermon progresses, until at last every member of the congregation knows that God means business with them personally. To begin with the personal and move towards the general and less specific is to let the congregation off the hook before the sermon ends and lose its major impact.

5. The preacher should respect the order of scripture in the arrangement of his points, unless there are very strong reasons for doing otherwise. If he is working *inside* the text and has divided it into three manageable sections, with a point for each one, the order of his points should be the same as the order which the text follows. The same is true for narrative, if the preacher is expounding a biblical story. Congregations can find it very confusing if the order is changed. To preserve it helps them to recognise the 'flow' or 'journey' of the sermon.

By this time the preacher has selected a text, done all the necessary background study to enable him to grasp its truth, identified the major points which the sermon will contain and arranged them in such an order so that the maximum impact is made on his hearers. He is now in a position to concentrate on the content of each point. Once again his chief concern is that the congregation will be able to grasp the truth which he is delivering and relate to it in a way which enables him to achieve his objective. It is clear, therefore, that each point must contain three major elements; *exposition, illustration and application*. He needs to identify these as he builds the sermon, but it is neither necessary nor advisable that these are announced to the congregation. Within each point he will lay bare the truth of scripture as his exposition, illustrate it and apply it to the lives of his hearers. The order in which these various elements are included within each point may, indeed ought to, vary in order to give the sermon some variety and retain the attention of his hearers. No point can be most effective unless it contains each of these elements.

The final element at this stage in the process is to return to the question which was mentioned earlier, "Is it necessary for the congregation to remember the points?" As we have said, in some cases this may be desirable but in most instances it is quite unnecessary. What matters is not that they remember each point, but that the final thrust of biblical truth makes an impact upon them. At one time preachers spent hours trying to get titles for their points which rhymed or where alliteration could be employed. It was almost always a complete waste of time. The journey of the preacher's argument, the flow of the sermon, are far more important than the points which he may wish to make.

As he eventually writes his sermon the preacher will remember that he is called to appeal to the mind, heart and will of his hearers. He will be aware that to appeal to the mind his deduction of truth, the progress in his argument and the insight which his background research has revealed are most important. The heart is not reached in that way. Here it is the senses which are most important. The preacher will, therefore, seek to paint a word picture in the minds of his hearers. He will use descriptive language and talk about what the characters saw, heard, smelt, tasted and felt; and all this is only possible because he has first got inside the story himself. If he can help the congregation to feel what the characters in the story felt he will have achieved his objective. Such an approach is not limited to biblical narrative. It can be used equally well with, say, the Psalms or the Epistles, but here the preacher will use his skill to paint a word picture of the writer or the original reader. We only realise the power of some biblical teaching when we remember the circumstances of those who wrote it and those who first read it. It is in describing their situation that the preacher will appeal to the heart of his listeners.

Through his appeal to both the mind and the heart the preacher will touch the will of his hearers so that, like those who knew the challenge of the gospel long ago, they will ask "What must we do?"

Practical Aspects of Sermon Preparation

Before long every preacher realises that he needs a strategy for sermon preparation. The busier a preacher is, the more important the strategy becomes. It can be frightening to know that one is expected to preach on a given Sunday but the subject of the sermon is unclear. The closer Sunday comes the more daunted the preacher feels. By Saturday night he is convinced that he ought to have given this more serious thought three weeks ago!

For this reason busy preachers need to work well in advance. The priority which the preacher gives to his ministry, both in the study and the pulpit, says much about his view of this great task. If he is going to do justice to his ministry, his people and his Lord he needs to prepare adequately, and for most people that means in plenty of time. The power of his delivery will be determined, to a large extent, by his familiarity with his material; and for this reason too he needs to allow himself adequate time for preparation.

The text from which he will preach will become clear. It will either be 'given' by the lectionary or preaching scheme, it will have chosen him or it will be one of his 'sermons on the stocks' which is approaching maturity. Once he has a text he needs to decide how he is going to approach it and do his initial preparation. This will involve getting to the heart of the text's message. He will need to do all the background reading he can and eventually the first bridge - from the Bible to the preacher - will be constructed. If the preacher has allowed adequate time for his preparation he will probably find that the sermon subject or text will be a background thought in his mind on which he will reflect whilst doing other things. He will make notes and jottings until the time comes for him to get all the available material together and commence the sermon structure. This should be no later than the beginning of the week before he is due to preach. He will now need to decide whether he is going to approach the text from 'outside' or 'inside' and the main points of the sermon will become clear. If the preacher has gathered far too much material for one sermon he will not be afraid to discard some knowing that his first calling is not to impart as much information as possible, but to enable an encounter between his hearers and the Lord. As the sermon begins to take shape the preacher will be conscious of his aim. Many find it helpful to write, at the top of the pages on which the preparation is done, "The aim of this sermon is to........" By the time he has finished this stage of his preparation the preacher should be able to summarize the content of his message in a single sentence which a child could understand. His attempts to do so will indicate both his clarity of thought and his precision in fulfilling the objectives of this sermon.

Supplementary Material

As well as the material which the preacher has discovered enabling him to give an accurate exposition of the text, supplementary material is required as well. Every point which he makes will need an illustration. There may also be helpful quotes and insights which other Christians have had on this same passage. To try and find all this material, from scratch, for each sermon is a very daunting task. Experienced preachers recognise the need to constantly gather such material and to have a system in which it can be stored and from which it can be easily retrieved.

For those who preach regularly sermon preparation becomes a way of life. Of course, there are particular times when it is the sole object of their attention, but they are always aware that the experiences in which they share, the things they observe, the books they read, the television programmes they watch and everything which they encounter could one day find its way into a sermon. In many respects the personal experiences of the preacher are the greatest source of illustrative material. In the telling of the personal story there is a genuine quality which can never be there with a story which has been borrowed from another. Of course, preachers do hear other preachers and there is a constant temptation to use an illustration which you have heard or read from someone else. Some wonder whether that is justifiable, and the answer is 'Yes, providing you acknowledge the source.' By doing so the power of the illustration is not diminished and the integrity of the preacher is safeguarded. To tell a story which you heard from another preacher as though it were your own is basically dishonest and no preacher of the gospel will seek to draw others to Christ by methods which compromise their own integrity.

Preachers will also find illustrative material in books and newspapers. If the newspaper is going to be discarded the selected story can be simply cut out for use later. If it is not at the head of the page the preacher will want to make a note of the particular paper together with the date so that when he uses it they can be quoted. When it comes to books that the preacher reads he will have to develop a way of retaining the material he may find. Some make a simple note as they read the book and then return to it later, write out the story or quote on a separate piece of paper and store it away. Others, if they are going to keep the book, recognise that this can be a long and laborious process. What the preacher needs at a later date is not necessarily the written quote, but an indication of where it may be found. For this reason, as the book is read he will have a small card which he may use as a bookmark. As he comes across something worth saving he will make a note of the subject and the page number. When the book is completed the preacher will re-write the card. On this 'new edition' he will have the subject, the title of the book and the page number all on one line. When the card is completed he will cut it into separate pieces so that each piece gives him the subject, the book's title and the page number. All these pieces can then be stored in the appropriate files for use later. If, at a subsequent date, he needs an illustration on 'discipleship', for example, he will look in the file and discover a number of cards with references to different books. It is then a comparatively simple task to find the most appropriate illustration for the sermon he is currently preparing.

It is clear that every preacher needs a filing system for this material. Most preachers find that such a system grows with their preaching career. They may begin with record cards in a shoe box. Before long this becomes inadequate and a system of files replace the cards. Experienced preachers may well have a whole filing cabinet of material on which they can draw. The important thing about any system is that the preacher can use it easily. He must know where a particular cutting ought to be stored and he must be able to retrieve it later when he needs it. The computer literate may feel comfortable with a data base whilst others may feel more comfortable with a shoe box. Whatever you use, if it does the job and you feel comfortable with it, stick with it. It is simply a tool at the preacher's disposal.

Most preachers file their material according to subject, but occasionally they may come across a story which may be illustrative of two subjects, depending on which aspect of the story is emphasised as it is told. It is not difficult, for example, to imagine a story which may illustrate either the call of God or the obedience of a disciple, depending on which way it is told. In such instances the preacher either provides two copies of the story or reference, placing each one in the appropriate file, or he adds a card with a cross reference. In the 'Call of God' file he would insert a card with the words "See also 'Obedience' file story of man on bus".

Some preachers have been known to file their material according to text. They will have a file devoted to each book of the Bible, sub-divided into chapters. When material is found which illustrates a particular verse they will note the verse on the cutting or record card and slip it into the file of the appropriate chapter. When they later come to preach on a particular verse they look in the file to see what they have! If this method works for you employ it, but most preachers find the subject files more appropriate.

Illustrations are invaluable in holding the congregation's attention and reinforcing the exposition. They root biblical truth in the world and concepts which the congregation know. However, one word of caution ought to be offered. An illustration ought to illustrate, i.e. it ought to make the point clearer. If it does not it may be a good story, but it is inappropriate in that place. The choice of suitable illustrations is one of the factors which will be considered as the preacher seeks to 'build the second bridge' between himself and the congregation. It is all too easy for a preacher to use an illustration which is clear to him, because it concerns a subject which he knows something about, but lost on the congregation because they do not share his personal interest. Some preachers have been known to share the story of obscure Greek myths believing them to be illustrations! In fact they did not illustrate the truth. They obscured it, simply because the congregation did not live in that world. A bad or inappropriate illustration is worse than no illustration at all.

One also needs to be sensitive to the moral, political and social outlook of the congregation. We may, in other ways, want to challenge some of the congregations presuppositions; but the illustration is not the place to do it. If the preacher tells a story to which the hearer takes exception the hearer spends the rest of the sermon either thinking about something else or quietly seething. The illustration has not captured his attention, it has lost it completely. All illustrations ought to point the congregation toward the biblical exposition. An inappropriate illustration points them away from it.

By now the sermon will really be taking shape. The subject, text, method of approach, structure, points, nuances of exposition, illustration and application are all becoming clear. But the sermon needs both a beginning and an ending, and both are of crucial importance. If we contrast the attention level of the preacher and the congregation as the sermon progresses we will quickly discover how important the introduction and conclusion really are. When the sermon begins the attention of the congregation is at its height, as the sermon proceeds it diminishes. Minds begin to wander and other matters compete for the hearer's concentration. When the preacher says 'And in conclusion....' they wake up again! In contrast the preacher gives most of his attention to the substance of his message. For him the introduction is simply a way into that, and the conclusion is a way out of it. In fact, therefore, when the preacher's concentration is at its greatest the hearer's is at its lowest. The astute preacher will, consequently, do all he can as he begins, and as he ends, to ensure that the congregation get the message. It is to a consideration of both the introduction and the conclusion that we must now turn.

The Introduction
When the congregation take their seats after the hymn or worship song and when the preacher moves to deliver the sermon he has approximately 30 seconds to win the attention of his people. If he does not win them then it will be increasingly difficult to do so later. For this reason alone every sermon introduction is of great importance.

Traditionally the Introduction has contained three elements; the announcement of the text, the announcement of the subject and an illustration which points the congregation towards the substance of the sermon. The order in which these elements occur may vary, but each one needs to be present. On some occasions it may be most appropriate to begin with the illustration, that will lead to the subject, and from the subject the preacher will point the congregation to the text. He can then proceed with his exposition. On other occasions the subject may come first, "This morning we are thinking about discipleship." Followed by the text, "Do you remember the words of Jesus from our scripture reading 'If any one would come after me....'?" A Further option is to announce the text first, follow it with a story and point to congregation to the rest of the sermon with the words, "This morning we are thinking about discipleship."

If the preacher is frequently occupying the same pulpit, variety is particularly important. A congregation can quickly become familiar with the formula followed by a particular preacher and, consequently, the impact of the sermon can be lost. Because the introduction to any sermon must arrest the attention of the hearers its vitality and relevance must be immediately plain. For this reason many of the most experienced preachers often begin with an illustration which then leads to the announcement of either the text or the subject.

The Conclusion
Many preachers find the conclusion the most challenging part of sermon preparation. They have a clear idea what they want to say, they even know how they are going to draw people into the subject; but they don't know how to finish. Campbell Morgan, that great prince of the pulpit said, "The conclusion must conclude, and in order to conclude well it must include, and in order to conclude perfectly it must preclude." Every preacher would do well to take his advice seriously.

We need to remember the purpose of the conclusion. It is to draw the sermon to an end with a final presentation of the Gospel truth. This may take the form of a challenge, a suggestion as to how they might reasonably respond or a rhetorical question which forces the truth home. In most cases it is quite inappropriate for the preacher to use the conclusion to merely repeat his points in a shortened form. Rather, he needs to use this opportunity to hammer home the central truth of his message. If he has successfully answered the question *"What is this text <u>really</u> about?"* he will know the substance of his conclusion. He must not introduce any new thought or material at this stage, but simply lay the truth which has formed the core of his message before his hearers. He can do so with an illustration, a question or an offer; but whatever form the conclusion takes it must be personal in character. The time for generalities has gone. It is now simply the hearer and His Lord, and the preacher has the extraordinary privilege of standing between the two.

Let's take an over-view of the sermon at this stage. A check list of questions may be helpful.

Introduction

What are the text, subject and opening illustration?
In what order will they come?

The Body of the Sermon

What is this text <u>really</u> about?
What are the main points?
How many points are there?
Should I see this sermon as an unfolding journey?
Do the points follow the same order as they come in the text?
Do the congregation need to remember or even know what the points are?
Are the points in the right order?
Do they appeal to the mind, heart and will?
What are the exposition, illustration and application for each point?
Can I summarise the core of this message in one sentence?

Conclusion

What is the core Gospel truth which I aim to hammer home?
Have I inadvertently included some new material?
Am I going to finish with a question, an illustration or an offer?
Is this personal, touching the soul of the hearer?

Preaching the Sermon

If we are to preach with power we need to understand clearly the contrast between a lecture and a sermon. We have already mentioned this, but it bears repeating at this point. We may have been mindful of this during all our preparation but if the sermon is delivered in a lecture style it undercuts all that we have said about the sermon's distinctive nature. It is a great mistake to feel that all the preparation which needs to be done is done in the study. Once that is completed and the sermon is written one kind of preparation is completed, but another is about to begin. It is the preparation required to deliver the sermon effectively, and it is at this point that some preachers fail to achieve their potential.

The preacher must aim to become as familiar as possible with his material. Many preachers, even though they may preach from brief notes, find it very helpful to type or write out a full sermon manuscript. Not only does this clarify the sermon construction in the preachers mind it also enables him to become very familiar with what he intends to say. It is wrong for the preacher to concentrate solely on his sermon material, for after all, that is merely an exposition of scripture. He must also seek to become as familiar as he can with the Bible passage. This will involve reading it many times in the version which he intends to use in the pulpit. As the service at which he will preach draws closer both the scripture passage and the sermon to be preached will become more and more a part of the preacher. He will find that he could almost recite the scripture passage from memory. He will have in his mind a clear picture of the overall shape of the sermon. He will know what he intends to say in the introduction; the expository points, illustrations and application points from the body of the sermon; and the content of the conclusion. If he sees the sermon as a journey rather than a number of distinct points he will have a clear grasp of the route which that journey is going to take.

Different preachers discover different ways of assisting this crucial process of becoming familiar with their material. Some use a tape recorder, reading the sermon onto a tape which can then be played back in the car or on any suitable occasion when the preacher is on his own. Many preachers find it most helpful to make brief notes of their main headings and illustrations on a postcard. Each point, each illustration will require only a word to jog the preacher's memory. He will write them down the left hand side of the postcard and at some convenient time he will go for a walk with the postcard in his pocket. He will go through the sermon in his mind and when he gets stuck the words on the postcard will serve as a much needed prompt. Some students of preaching have been known to speak the sermon out loud on such walks. In fact, cows residing in the fields adjacent to some notable Bible colleges have heard so many sermons it's a wonder they haven't been converted!

Every preacher recognises that, important though his delivery is, he alone is not able to achieve his objective. The Holy Spirit has been at work through the preacher's preparation and he needs to be at work through the preaching of the sermon and in the hearts of the hearers. If any conviction is to be wrought, if any good thing is to result from this exposition, it will be the Holy Spirit's work. For this reason alone the preacher will endeavour to soak the whole matter in prayer. He will lift his own efforts before the Lord. He will seek that 'power from on high' as he preaches. If he knows his congregation well he will picture them sitting in worship as he preaches, and he will pray for them individually.

The question of whether to preach from a full manuscript, notes or to rely on one's memory is often asked by preachers seeking to improve their skill. Several matters need to be taken into account in order to answer this question:

1. Unlike the actor, the preacher does not need to be word-perfect. He prepared what he is going to say. He will say it. If he gets a word wrong here and there no one will know. For the preacher the important issue is not whether he sticks to his manuscript perfectly but whether he faithfully delivers the truth which the Lord has laid in his heart from the scriptures.

2. Preaching is 'communication through personality', to use Philips Brooks' phrase. If the preached message is to be declared with power and receive a ready welcome in the hearts of his hearers the preacher needs to 'live' the message and let the message live as he declares it. Nothing kills power in the pulpit like a slavish adherence to a written manuscript. If the preacher is 'tied to his notes' all eye contact is lost. He is more concerned about saying the right thing than letting the message live through him. The air accompanying his delivery is more suited to a lecture than a sermon. For these reasons any preacher seeking to improve his skill ought to endeavour to wean himself away from a slavish adherence to a full manuscript. Preaching involves developing a rapport with the congregation so that the message can be communicated effectively. The preacher must constantly be sensitive to the feed-back which he is getting from the hearers. To be tied to one's notes kills any such rapport.

3. Whatever notes the preacher has with him in the pulpit need to be clearly written and easily read at the distance which the pulpit demands. They ought also to be as inconspicuous as possible. This raises a number of issues: Should the notes be written or typed? What size should the paper be? Where should they be placed? If a preacher needs any notes at all and if, when he glances down at them, he cannot clearly read them, he has lost eye contact with his congregation and any relationship which he was building with them. It may only take a second or two to try and read a word in your notes which is not clear, but that is quite long enough to be a distraction to the

congregation. Further, if the notes are written or typed on A4 paper everyone in the congregation can see them. There are few pulpit desks big enough to take a Bible and two sheets of A4 side by side. This means that at the end of each sheet the preacher must readjust his notes and everyone knows he's doing it. It is another distraction. Worse, if he writes on both sides of the paper his progress through his material is even more obvious. No preacher seeking to improve his delivery should use A4 paper written on both sides, or even one side. The notes need to be as inconspicuous as possible whilst still meeting the preacher's needs.

There is a way round this. Any notes should be written on paper no larger than A5. If the notes are closer than the reading desk in the pulpit they can be written smaller and so less sheets of paper are required. If the preacher needs a substantial manuscript he can write or type it on A4 paper folded in half to make A5. If he prepares his notes in such a way that the folded A4 paper makes a little booklet he can insert that between the pages of his Bible and secure it over the spine of the Bible with a rubber band. He can then hold his Bible in his hand throughout the sermon, consulting his notes when necessary. This brings the notes closer to the preacher's eye, makes them less conspicuous and even when he needs to consult them it is far less distracting for the congregation.

Every preacher knows how substantial his notes need to be to enable his delivery to be effective, but as his skill improves he should endeavour to become less reliant on a full manuscript. Many preachers find this a daunting prospect, but it is not as difficult as it sounds. Let us imagine that the preacher has prepared adequately, typed or written a full manuscript on the size of paper recommended and made a summary card from those notes. If he feels that he needs the full manuscript in the pulpit let him underline the main headings and key words or phrases with a red pen or mark them with a highlighter. This will enable him to become less dependant on the manuscript. He may realize, after a while, that if all he needs are the key words or phrases there is little point in having the rest with him in the pulpit. He can now contemplate using the summary card instead. This is a great step forward and the transition is best made when he is preaching a sermon with which he has become really familiar. The first time he does it he takes a risk, but his confidence begins to grow. He begins to discover a new freedom in his preaching as he is set free from his notes. It's an act of faith and God honours it. After a while he may begin to feel that the notes on the summary card need not be quite as full as he has been using. Maybe he could preach from headings alone; one word to remind him of the introduction, one word for each point and one word for the conclusion. Many preachers feel that such an ideal is for too ambitious for them, but with care and perseverance it is possible to rely less and less on one's notes, and so attain greater and greater freedom in ones preaching.

Some experienced preachers even discard the summary card. They may keep it in their Bible for easy reference just before they preach, but then move it to just within the back cover. It's still there, like a safety net if they get stuck, but they aim not to consult it at all. Some preachers, who have developed a particular expository style, will mark the text in the Bible with different colours, each one representing either the main points or sub-headings. They have their own colour code and it sets them free from additional notes altogether. This clearly demonstrates that as a preacher's experience grows he can know a greater liberty in his preaching by relying less on his notes. He may, in time, develop his own system of memory jogging aids. So much the better. What really matters is that the message gets across and the enthusiastic preacher will do all he can to improve his skill.

In the vestry, before the service, the preacher should read his notes through quietly for the last time before he preaches. He will want to pay particular attention to the 'flow' of the sermon so that he has a last, clear picture in his mind of the route which his message is going to take.

During the hymn before the sermon he will be remembering that he has just thirty seconds to win his congregation's attention, so he will want his opening three sentences in his mind. When the hymn ends exactly how is he going to begin? Is he going to lead in a short prayer at that point? What are the first words of the sermon going to be? Being careful to maintain eye-contact he will begin, and as the sermon flows he will be surprised how God honours his faith.

We need to say something about the use of the voice. Of course the preacher needs to be clearly audible and, if a public address system is in operation, he needs to know how to use it. But more important than that, the preacher needs to recognise that the voice is one of the most effective tools at his disposal. The congregation are going to be captured, not just by what the preacher says, but by the way in which he says it. The unalterable rule ought to be that the tone and volume of the voice ought to be appropriate for the words he is saying. For example, the effective preacher would never say 'Jesus said, "My peace I give to you"' in a raucus tone or with excessive volume. The meaning of the words spoken demands a gentle tone and a quiet delivery. On the other hand, to speak about the disciples receiving power when the Holy Spirit comes upon them demands a quite different use of the preacher's voice. Throughout his delivery the astute preacher will use his voice in a way which reflects the content of his message in both volume and tone.

Gesture also needs to reinforce the message, not distract from it. Many people talk with their hands, even on the phone! Gesture is part of the communication process. The preacher ought to be natural in the delivery of the sermon, and if his gesture is a natural out-flow of his personality God will be able to use it, but it needs to be handled with care. If the preacher is aware that his supreme calling is to give God the glory through his ministry all will be well. Normally gesture is not a problem, unless the preacher is seeking some glory for himself. If he is, the gestures reveal it, the congregation knows and all that the preacher hopes to achieve is undermined.

If the preacher is not relying heavily on a written manuscript he will discover a liberty in his preaching, yet he needs to be aware of the dangers inherent in this freedom. He may get carried away and preach for far too long or he may find himself being led by another train of thought which is really quite unproductive. In order to safeguard his ministry he needs to impose a self-discipline which some do not find easy. Yet there are advantages too, in addition to those already mentioned. It may be that as he preaches a new and more appropriate illustration comes to mind. If this happens he ought to use it. It may well be God's word for a particular situation in that congregation. However, if he is about to tell a story which has just entered his mind let him be sure he knows how it will end before he begins to tell it. There can be few more embarrassing moments than the discovery that, on the spur of the moment, you have begun to tell a story but you cannot remember the punch line.

Many great preachers of a former generation used to place particular emphasis on the conclusion of the sermon, as well as its introduction. They would have the various elements of the conclusion quite clear in the mind; and they would know exactly what their last words would be. We have much to learn from them. Every preacher ought to be quite clear how the sermon is going to end. Some say 'Amen'. Some lead in a short prayer. Discover a way which is right for you. Use it, but don't be restricted by it. Variety is important here as well. Sometimes to leave a congregation with a simple question as the last word might be right. Sometimes a repetition of the text. Sometimes for the preacher just to stop and remain still for five seconds is the most powerful way to make sure the message hits the target. Whatever way he chooses the preacher must know that when the last word is spoken his work is done. The gospel has been faithfully proclaimed. The Holy Spirit has done His work. It is now out of the preacher's hands. He must leave it with the Lord and the people, knowing that nothing ever offered in the Master's service is wasted.

Preaching for a Verdict

There is a sense in which all expository preaching is preaching for a verdict. Whenever the truth of scripture is presented to people in a way which they can readily understand it confronts them with a challenge. The preacher will expect to see the evidence of the congregation's response to that challenge. Normally this will be found in a deepening of their devotion or a change in their attitude, behaviour or life-style. There is little point in presenting the gospel if there is no expectation of response.

However, it cannot be denied that there are specific occasions when it may be advisable for the preacher to seek a definite response from his congregation there and then. He will catch a sense that everything about the service or meeting has been working towards this point. The challenge of the gospel is so intense that it would be quite wrong for him not to provide the opportunity for his hearers to register their positive response to it. The means whereby they do so is commonly called 'the appeal'. We are using the term here to include the wide variety of forms which that appeal may take, although we will discuss these in greater detail later. Every preacher of the gospel who is faithful to his calling will, therefore, from time to time, find himself asking, "Should I make an appeal?" and if he concludes that he should he will want to know the form it should take and how to do it.

Why should I consider making an appeal?
In order to answer this question the preacher will want to take a number of factors into account.

The nature of the service or event is very significant. Some events are organised with the specific intention of bringing people to a new depth of Christian commitment. In the local church there may be a series of services working towards a climax. It would be quite wrong in such a situation not to provide the opportunity for people to register their response. There may be a particular opportunity offered by, say, an evangelistic event. There too, there ought to be the mechanism to enable people to respond positively to the gospel.

Closely allied to this is the *expectation of the people.* If a team of Christians have been working hard, maybe over many months, on a programme of evangelism or Christian discipleship they expect that an opportunity for response ought to be given at the concluding service or celebration. If it were not they would feel let down and cheated. In such a situation an appeal of some kind seems as natural as it would seem alien to many regular acts of worship.

The season of the Christian year is also a factor which the preacher will wish to take into account. There can be no time when it is always wrong to make an appeal, just as there is no time when it is always right; but we must acknowledge that there are Christian festivals which draw our attention to the heart of the gospel in a particular way. Easter is a prime example. After preaching on the work of Christ on a cross it may be quite natural to call people, as it were, to the foot of that cross in penitence and faith. After preaching on the resurrection it may be quite natural to invite members of the congregation to enter the new life which his rising makes possible. If Pentecost is an offer to disciples today, as well as those who gathered in Jerusalem so many years ago, the preacher may want to help his people experience the infilling of the Holy Spirit for themselves. An appeal may be the most natural way of doing this.

Added to all these factors we must take *God's guidance to the preacher* very seriously. This is almost impossible to define, yet it cannot be denied. If the preacher is one who seeks to walk closely to the Lord, if he has made the service and all his preparation a matter of prayer, if as he preaches there is an awareness that God is at work amongst the people; he may know a deep inner sense that this is what he ought to do. An inward imperative drives him on. He knows that not to have an appeal in this situation would simply be disobedience.

In seeking to discover whether he should make an appeal a preacher will want to take all these factors into account. However, a word of caution may not come amiss. Every preacher should avoid reaching a decision about this on the spur of the moment, especially whilst he is preaching. Even though we have acknowledged God's guidance to the preacher we must also acknowledge that this guidance is given before the preacher enters the pulpit as well as whilst he is preaching. We hope so, or all his preparation is in vain! So, even if divine guidance is the major factor there ought to have been a growing sense in the preacher's heart that this may be what he ought to do. He may not be able to say definitely, before the service begins, whether he is going to make an appeal or not but he should at least be able to say, "Unless I receive strong guidance to the contrary whilst I preach I intend to make an appeal", or "I do not intend to make an appeal" as the case may be.

Ill thought-out, badly conducted appeals for which there has been no preparation and following which there is no follow-up are a disgrace to the gospel. They give all appeals a bad name, give our people a jaundiced view of anything which may challenge them and undermine any future attempts which may be made to invite a response. They must be avoided at all costs. But where the preparation has been careful, where the appeal is conducted with sincerity and reverence, and where the support given to those who respond is loving, it can be one of the most effective ways of enabling ordinary people to enter into a new dimension of Christian living or obedience.

What should I do?
There are a number of ways in which people can signify their response to the challenge of the gospel. Broadly speaking, these can be divided into three groups.

Those seeking a response following the close of the service or meeting.
These include inviting those who wish to ask the preacher for a Decision Card or booklet, inviting them to remain in their seats when everyone else has left, inviting them to signify their response to the preacher in a private conversation or inviting them to attend a meeting at a later time which is specifically designed to help them.

Those seeking a public response without coming forward.
These include inviting those responding to raise their hands, catching the preacher's eye whilst other pray, standing in their seats whilst others remain seated or shouting out a simple phrase which the preacher suggests e.g. "Christ for me!"

Those seeking a public response signified by coming forward to the front of the church.
These include inviting those responding to come and shake hands with the preacher, stand at the front of the church facing the communion table, moving straight to a counselling room or coming to kneel at the communion rail.

A slight, but significant variation of this method which has grown in popularity in recent years is the 'altar call'. This is far more common in the United States where, in some churches it is recognised as the normal practice at every service. Members of the congregation are invited, during a hymn, to come and kneel at the communion rail, say their prayers, make their peace with God, open their lives to His power and then, as the congregation continue to sing, make their way back to the place where they were standing. This can be most effective and on occasions can result in people coming to the communion rail, praying quietly and returning throughout the hymn. If this method is employed it does mean that those who respond are not expected to be involved in any private prayer or ministry following the appeal, although that could be offered in addition to the altar call if it were thought advisable. If the preacher decides on an altar call rather than the more conventional appeal, where those who respond are expected to be involved in prayer or personal ministry later, he needs to make this clear at the time of making the appeal.

There are things which could be said for and against each of these methods and our views are no doubt coloured by our experience of their success or failure. Here we will not attempt an evaluation of each one, but we can make some general observations which the preacher should take into account when deciding which method to use.

1. The person conducting the appeal needs to take the physical situation into account. For example; it is no use asking the congregation to look up and catch your eye if you cannot see them all. It is no use asking people to leave their seats and come to the front of the church if they cannot physically get out whilst the other seats are occupied. The person making the appeal needs to ensure that it is physically possible for people to respond in the way he requests.

2. It is morally indefensible to ask people to do something easy and then ask the same people to do something more difficult. For example, one should never ask people to silently invite Christ into their hearts whilst everyone prays, and then ask those who have done so to raise their hands, and then ask those who have raised their hands to come forward. Such practices are, rightly, perceived to be manipulation and place the motives of the preacher in considerable doubt.

3. There ought to be a harmony between the nature of the response and the gospel challenge. To come and kneel at a communion rail says much about the nature of the response which that person is making. This is of a quite different tone to shouting out or even standing up in one's seat. One speaks of penitence and humble submission whilst the other says, "Count me in!" There may be occasions when both these moods are appropriate, but their applicability in a given situation will depend on the character of the message to which they are signifying a response.

4. Once the preacher has decided which method he is going to use he needs to think the whole matter through very carefully. He will want to be clear about the point in the service where it is going to take place, what the rest of the congregation will be doing at the time, how those wishing to respond will actually do so, what assistance he may need if the response is of a large number, what will happen to those who have responded both immediately following the appeal and later. When all this is clear in his mind he can approach the appeal with a confidence which the congregation will recognise and which will put them at ease. If the preacher feels comfortable with what he is doing he will seek to help his congregation to feel comfortable with it too.

How should I do it ?

The moment when, through the preached word, individual members of the congregation feel the call of God is infinitely precious. It is a moment when life's direction is changed and it is of eternal consequence. Those in the congregation who are experiencing God's call have one question uppermost in their minds, "What do I need to do to respond to this?" It is the preachers task now to make that plain and to enable them to do so with reverence and dignity. He will best do this by following two simple guiding principles -

1. He will seek to remove anything which may be a barrier to their response. Embarrassment, uncertainty about what they are letting themselves in for and wondering how they will appear to others are the most common. The preacher, therefore needs to reassure them that what he is asking them to do is the natural consequence of the message which they have heard. If the message has confronted them with a choice, if the moment of decision has arrived, the preacher's task is to help them understand how their inward desire to respond can be met by answering to the appeal. Each preacher will have his own way of doing this. He may want to speak a reassuring word pointing out the value of honouring God before men. He may appeal to the heart and speak of the constraining love of God drawing them to himself. He may seek to identify the sacredness of their response with the sacredness of the communion rail at which they are invited to kneel. There is no right way for every preacher and every situation. It is clear, however, that the preacher needs to give this matter significant consideration prior to the event. A faltering attitude or lack of clarity on his part will not remove barriers for the hearers, it will construct them.

2. Secondly the preacher needs to make it absolutely plain what he is asking them to do, when, where, how and why. Most bad appeals fail at this point. The preacher is filled with enthusiasm and good intentions, but he makes too many assumptions, particularly with congregations where appeals are not the norm. He thinks they know what to do but they are left with terrible uncertainties. How can they respond if they do not know how to do it? The whole procedure needs to be explained with crystal clarity. In order to give these specific instructions the preacher needs to have thought out the whole procedure very clearly before the service or meeting. Does the appeal take place during a hymn? Will all those who wish to, be able to respond no matter what part of the building they are occupying? Do some, because of their location, need more specific instructions? Is he asking them to signify their response by standing, coming forward, catching his eye etc.? If they are being asked to come forward are they being invited to stand at the front? Which way round? Are they being asked to kneel at the communion rail? Should they bring their hymn books with them so they can continue to sing? Should they kneel, or stand, in prayer? What instructions need to be given to others who may have come to the service with them? When they have responded what is going to happen to them? Are they expected to be interviewed or receive ministry from a pastoral or counselling team? Or are these options simply being made available should they wish to receive them? After the hymn will there be a prayer of dedication led by the preacher? Will those who have responded then be free to return to their seats? All these questions need to be answered because they will be in the minds of the congregation. Each one removes a barrier and enables the response for which both the preacher and the Lord long.

Several other questions need to be addressed.

Should the preacher stop the hymn between verses to renew the appeal?
Once again there is no definitive answer to this question, but a few guiding principles may help. There are two main dangers which the preacher must avoid. One is to drag the appeal out until someone, usually out of desperation, responds. The other is to give the impression that he is seeking a response at all costs. It is clear to the congregation, in such situations, that this has far more to do with the preacher's ego than the Lord's glory. For both these reasons a simple rule of thumb is offered. Never stop a hymn more than once, and never stop a hymn before someone has responded. If the preacher follows this guidance he will earn the respect of his hearers, which in itself enables them to respond when the time is right for them. Congregations are sickened by the stopping of an appeal hymn over and over again. It does not enable them to respond. It alienates them. The preacher should only stop the hymn after there has been a response because that is clear evidence that God's spirit is at work amongst His people. It is to Him that they are responding, not to the preacher.

What does the preacher do when the hymn is over?
If those who have responded have never witnessed anything like this before they will be wondering what to do when the hymn is finished. They may be very emotional. Tears are by no means uncommon. They need to know that someone is in control of the situation, and that someone is the preacher. He needs to be sensitive to the solemnity of that moment, but at the same time his instructions need to be clear and easily understood. It would be usual for the preacher to lead in a prayer of dedication, especially for those who have responded, and then issue clear instructions to both those who have responded and those who have them in their care. By demonstrating that he is clearly in control the preacher enables this moment to be a milestone in the spiritual lives of those answering the appeal. To fumble at this point robs them of something infinitely precious and persuades them that they are never going to do that again!

It is almost invariably better to have those who have responded move back to their seats or to an anteroom for counselling during the singing of a hymn or worship song. If the preacher has not arranged this with the musicians prior to the service he may feel that the most convenient way of proceeding is to sing the last verse of the appeal hymn again. In any case, this preserves the atmosphere of the moment. Following the singing of that verse or worship song the preacher will lead in a short prayer of blessing on the congregation, maybe the Grace, and the service will be over.

What if no one responds?
There may be many preachers who are reluctant to make an appeal because they are fearful that no one will respond. This reveals the preacher's faulty perspective

and it needs to be sorted out. Every preacher ought to be quite clear where his responsibilities begin and end. To prepare adequately, to walk close enough to the Lord to know His guidance, to preach with authority, to commend his Saviour; all these are rightly the preacher's responsibility. The inner work of grace, the response of the congregation to the message, the movement of God's Holy Spirit amongst His people; these do not belong to the preacher's care. If lives are changed as a result of his preaching he needs to be careful that the glory goes to the Lord. Ego can so easily find a way into even the consecrated heart. If the gospel which he proclaims seems unpalatable to the people the preacher ought not to apologise, providing the faith he proclaims is that which was once and for all delivered unto the saints. The content of the gospel, as well as the response which it receives are not the preacher's responsibility.

If any preacher decides, under the guidance of God, to make an appeal he needs to be quite clear that when his last word is said and the congregation rise to sing the last hymn his responsibilities are faithfully discharged. He has offered it to the Lord, and it is then in the Lord's hand. The preacher needs to stand back and see the constraining Spirit of God at work in the congregation. Sometimes they will not respond, and there can be many reasons for this. If they do not the preacher must not feel downhearted or foolish for doing what God told him to do. He fulfilled his responsibilities and if the people do not register an outward response to the message it is not his fault. Often they will and every preacher involved in ministry of this kind is overwhelmed by the graciousness of God as he sees ordinary people being constrained by the love of God. The best advice to every preacher is this, "Be obedient, no matter what the consequences. After all you are answerable to God, not your critics!"

What will happen to those who have responded?
This matter needs to be handled with sensitivity and great care. If there are those who have registered a response to Christ they will need to be fed into a discipleship programme of some kind. If there are those who have known a deeper work of grace they will need continuing support. If, however, there are those who have responded to an altar call and returned to their seats they may resent any prying questions. If they had recognised their need for private prayer or counsel they would have availed themselves of it at the time of the appeal. In these cases the preacher must exercise his continuing pastoral ministry and simply be grateful to God for what He has done. If the preacher who has made the appeal to which people have responded is not the Minister of that local church, the Minister who has the people in his pastoral care must be informed.

The nature of the gospel demands that on occasions every preacher preaches for a verdict. Let him be faithful to his calling. Let him never be afraid to commend his Saviour. Let him faithfully seek a response from his people as the Lord directs him.

God will honour his faithfulness. Today there are thousands of people in the Christian Church who were brought to a point of commitment to Christ through an evangelistic appeal. Thousands more knew the call of God to service in a specific area through the appeal made by a preacher. The evidence speaks for itself. God honours this way of bringing people to Himself, and he will honour it through the ministry of every faithful preacher.

And Finally.....

The authority of the preacher lies not in his power of persuasion, or any natural ability which he may posses, but in the authority which a gracious God has bestowed upon His word. He has promised that if His word goes forth it will not return until is has accomplished that which was intended. Sometimes God grants us to see the word accomplishing its work. On other occasions we never see it. Preachers have lived and died not knowing what their ministry has accomplished. But God knows, and that's all that matters.

One of the greatest blessings any preacher can know is to encounter someone who reports that they were present when he preached many years before, and that occasion was a turning point in their life. It not only warms the soul of the preacher, but it renews his confidence that a Sovereign Lord is in charge, and He will do his work, even though we may never know about it.

What better advice could be given to any preacher that that which Paul gave to Timothy: "Preach the Word, be prepared in season and out of season; correct, rebuke and encourage - with great patience and careful instruction" (2 Tim 4:2).

May every preacher glory in the privilege of revealing the Living Word, from the written word, by the spoken word.

Useful Addresses

CLIFF COLLEGE
Cliff Lane, Calver, Hope Valley, Derbys S32 3XG   Tel: 01246 582321
Helpful courses for preachers are often held at Cliff College. Enquiries should be addressed to the Administrative Officer.

THE COLLEGE OF PREACHERS,
81 North Road, Bourne, Lincs PE10 9BT   Tel: 01778 422929
The College of Preachers provides an ecumenical resource centre for preachers. They now run preaching courses to higher degree level and are happy to run courses on a variety of aspects of preaching to preachers' meetings.

Methodist Evangelicals Together
is the largest independent organisation in British Methodism today, uniting and representing evangelicals at every level within our denomination.

Our three core purposes are:
- **ADVOCATING:** Promoting and representing evangelicalism within Methodism, and Wesleyan evangelicalism within the wider evangelical world.
- **EQUIPPING:** Providing resources through publications, conferences and our website for evangelicals within British Methodism.
- **SUPPORTING:** Offering pastoral support and advice to evangelicals, who can often feel isolated within Methodism and face particular pressures.

MET is a fellowship for every Methodist who shares our desire to:
- Uphold the authority of Scripture
- Seek Spiritual Renewal
- Pray for Revival
- Spread Scriptural holiness
- Emphasise the centrality of the Cross

MET promotes partnership in the Gospel to proclaim Jesus as Lord. Our partners include:
- Cliff College
- ECG
- Share Jesus International
- Inspire Network

Join MET and partner with us to:
- *Network with evangelical Methodists in prayer and action.*
- *Add your voice to over 2000 others on key issues at all levels of the Methodist Church and beyond.*
- *Participate in national and local events.*
- *Receive the MET Connexion Magazine.*

Find us at:
www.methodistevangelicals.org.uk

or write to us
c/o Moorleys Print & Publishing, 23 Park Road, Ilkeston, Derbys DE7 5DA
who will pass on your valued enquiry.